It was the first day back at school after Christmas. The class buzzed with excitement. Lots of people had new pens for Christmas. Everyone was writing.

Invisible ink pens were lots of fun. You couldn't see what they wrote. When you scribbled over the writing with a pen, the words appeared like magic.

"Dear Sam," wrote Jo, "I got this pen for Christmas. It's really cool. It writes with invisible ink!"
Sam looked at the note. He held it up to the light bulb. He couldn't see any writing at all! Then he scribbled over it with a green pen. The words appeared like magic!

Sam borrowed Jo's invisible ink pen. He wrote, "What did you get for Christmas, Kim?"
Kim scribbled over the note and read it.
"I got an invisible ink pen, too," she said. "It's in my bag. What did you get?"

"Hey!" Ravi said, "Someone's got my new invisible ink pen!"
"Not me!" said Sam, shrugging his shoulders. "I borrowed Jo's pen."
"Not me!" said Kim, shrugging her shoulders. "My pen's in my bag."
"Quick, give me back my pen," said Jo. "Here comes Mrs Squire."

"Hello, class," said Mrs Squire, the science teacher. "In our science class this year, we are going to learn about electricity. Today we'll make our own electrical circuits."

"Cool!" Sam said with a big grin. He liked to make things. An electrical circuit would be fun to make.

"A circuit is a path for electricity to flow through," said Mrs Squire. She showed the class how to make an electrical circuit. She connected a wire to a battery, a buzzer and a light bulb.
"Now make your own electrical circuits," she said.

Soon the electrical circuits were working like magic. Buzzers buzzed and light bulbs flashed. Then the bell went for breaktime. "Well done!" said Mrs Squire. "You have all done very well."

Then suddenly, Kim sprang up…
"My pen's missing!" she said.
"So is mine!" said Jo.
"And so is mine," said Ravi. "It's been missing all morning!"
"Three missing pens!" said Sam. "We must have an invisible ink pen thief!"

"Let's set a trap to catch the thief," said Sam. "I've got a plan!" When no one was looking, Sam put his bag on his table. He connected the electrical circuit to his bag. When the bag was moved, the pins touched each other. This made the buzzer buzz and the light bulb flash.

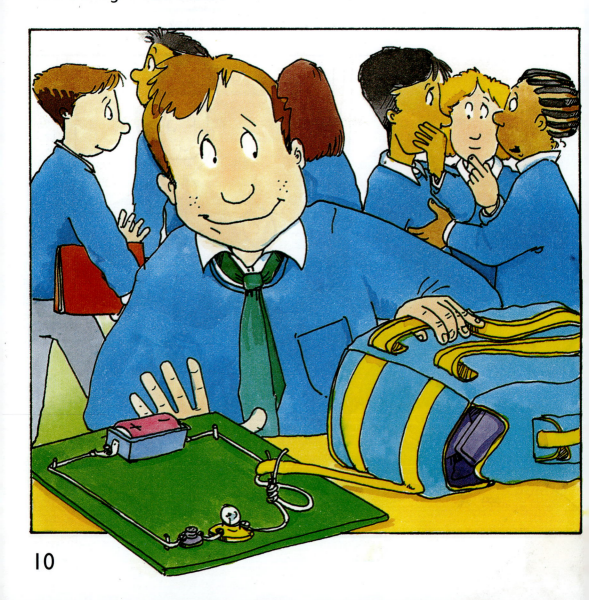

Then Sam said in a loud voice so that everyone could hear, "I got a really good invisible ink pen for Christmas. It's in my bag. I'll show it to you after breaktime. Come on, let's go and play football."

Kim and Sam hid outside until everyone had gone.
"What do we do now?" asked Kim.
"We go back inside and hide until the thief comes," said Sam.

They hid under Mrs Squire's table. They waited and waited and waited. At last the door opened. *Who* was it? Sam couldn't see. Kim couldn't see. They couldn't see, but they could hear. They could hear… *footsteps*.

Tip-tap, tip-tap!
The footsteps crossed the room. They seemed to stop at Sam's table. Sam and Kim stayed very still. They did not make a sound.

Someone was moving Sam's bag! The pins touched each other and electricity flowed through the wires.

It was like magic. The buzzer buzzed! The light bulb flashed! Sam and Kim sprang up.
"*Got you!*" they shouted.

It was Mrs Squire!
"Oh, there you are!" she said. "You know that you shouldn't put your bag on the table, Sam. That circuit works well. Well done!"

"We *still* don't know who the thief is!" said Kim.

Just then Ravi ran in.

"Aren't you coming to play football?" he said. "Come on!"

"Can't!" said Sam. "We want to catch the thief who took your invisible ink pen."

"What?" said Ravi. "I found my pen! It was on Jo's table."

"Hey!" said Jo. "That's *my* pen!"
"No, it's not!" said Ravi.
"Yes, it is!" said Jo.
"Then what's that in your pocket?" said Ravi.

"Oops!" said Jo. "Sorry! My pen was in my pocket all the time!"
"But where's *my* pen?" said Kim. "It's still missing! I'm sure I put it in my bag this morning."
"Are you really, really sure?" said Ravi.
"I think so…" said Kim.
Just then the bell rang.
"We'll look for it after school," said Sam. "Come on."

After school, Sam and Kim raced to Kim's house. Kim's mum was in the kitchen. The twins were playing at the kitchen table.
"Have you seen my invisible ink pen, Mum?" asked Kim.
"No, dear," said Mum.
"Oops!" said Ben.
"Oops!" said Jenny.

Sam looked at Kim. Kim looked at Sam. Then they both looked at the twins. Ben had something in his hand. It was Kim's pen!

"I like to draw," said Ben.
"I like to draw, too!" said Jenny. "We've drawn on *everything*!"
"My pen!" said Kim. "It was my own brother and sister all the time!"

"It wasn't an invisible ink pen thief," said Sam with a grin. "It was *two* invisible ink pen thieves!"